DOGS

Contents

S0-AQL-776

What is a dog?

Dogs vary more in their size and appearance than any other animal. But whether they are big or small, they all have good sight, very good hearing, and an excellent sense of smell.

Dogs have large, sharp, hard teeth.

The ribs form a strong cage.

On tip toe

Dogs walk on their toes. Tough toe pads and claws help them to grip. Dogs cannot pull their claws in.

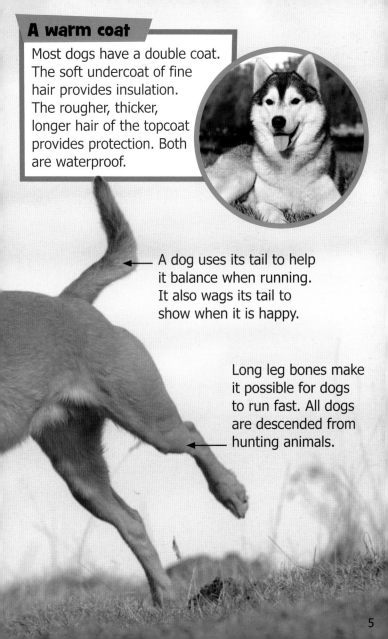

A warm coat

Most dogs have a double coat. The soft undercoat of fine hair provides insulation. The rougher, thicker, longer hair of the topcoat provides protection. Both are waterproof.

A dog uses its tail to help it balance when running. It also wags its tail to show when it is happy.

Long leg bones make it possible for dogs to run fast. All dogs are descended from hunting animals.

The dog family

Red Fox

When we talk about a dog, we usually mean a pet, but there are a number of wild members of the dog family, such as wolves, jackals, coyotes, foxes and dingoes.

The fox has a slim, strong body.

Members of the dog family

Wolf

Jackal

Dhole

The pointed ears move to pick up sounds. Foxes have very good hearing.

The fox's large, forward-facing eyes give it excellent eyesight.

The long, bushy tail helps with balance when the fox is running and jumping.

Hunting in packs

Wolves live together in groups of up to 20. These packs can kill animals much larger than themselves by hunting together. They also protect each other and share the care of their pups.

Coyote

Pet dogs

Dogs were the first animals to be domesticated, or tamed and treated as pets. You find pet dogs wherever you find people. Over the years, people have developed about 400 breeds of dogs that are good at a range of different things.

Afghan puppy

The Afghan hound is an old breed of hunting dog. It helped people to catch other animals when hunting.

Mixed breeds

If dogs from different breeds mate, the puppies are called mixed breeds, or mongrels. Mixed breeds are strong, healthy dogs, but until the puppy grows up, it is hard to know what it will be like.

The Afghan is a sight hound. (See page 10.)

Leader of the pack

Dogs are pack animals. They are happy for people to become the leader of their pack and tell them what to do.

Sight hounds

Hounds are dogs that are good at hunting other animals. Some hounds can see particularly well and hunt by sight. They keep the other animal in view and sprint to catch it. They are tall, lean, athletic-looking dogs with an elegant trot.

Did you know?

Greyhounds are amazing sprinters. They can run as fast as 45 mph (72 kph).

Long, strong legs help greyhounds to run at great speeds.

Well-known sight hounds

Whippet

Borzoi

Greyhound

The large eyes face forwards.

The greyhound's slight body means it does not carry much weight.

Sight hounds have deep chests and large lungs, so that they can keep running.

The shoulders swing freely so that the dog can take long strides.

Saluki

Scent hounds

Scent hounds are hunting dogs that have a particularly good sense of smell. They use this to follow the animals they are chasing. Scent hounds cannot sprint as fast as sight hounds, but they are able to keep running for a long time. Most scent hounds hunt in packs.

A mouth to smell

Scent hounds have a big mouth and this helps them follow a scent. The loose, moist folds of skin around the mouth pick up scent particles and send messages to the brain.

Basset Hound

Well-known scent hounds

Dachshund

Basset Hound

Bloodhound

Scent hounds mostly use their noses when tracking an animal. They can even follow a scent through water.

Scent hounds usually have drop ears. This means that their hearing is not as good as that of a dog with pointed, erect ears.

The large nose has deep, open nostrils.

The beagle has strong legs, so that it can keep going during a long hunt.

Beagle

Gundogs

Gundogs help people when they are out hunting. They are very intelligent, trainable dogs and are keen to please. Retrievers will run and fetch an animal that has been shot, wherever it happens to land.

Retrievers have a soft mouth. This means that they can carry a dead bird in their mouth without biting into it.

All dogs can swim. But retrievers are trained to leap into water and swim to collect a bird that has been shot.

Golden Retriever

Springer Spaniels

Spaniels are good at chasing birds out of the bushes.

Pointers

When pointers realize where an animal is hiding, they stand very still and point their nose towards it.

Gundogs make good companions. They are very active dogs and need a lot of exercise.

Setters

When it is hunting, a setter figures out where the bird is and sends it flying up in the sky so that the hunter can shoot it.

Terriers

Terriers are tough, brave dogs that hunt on their own and are not afraid of being hurt. They will chase rats and foxes above ground and follow them down tunnels under the ground.

Jack Russell terriers are about 1 ft (30 cm) tall. They were bred to chase foxes from their burrows.

Some terriers have a smooth coat, while others have a wiry coat.

Jack Russell terriers are full of energy.

Jack Russell terriers have strong claws, which makes it easier for them to dig.

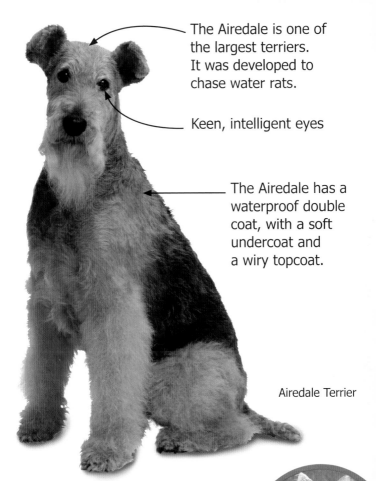

The Airedale is one of the largest terriers. It was developed to chase water rats.

Keen, intelligent eyes

The Airedale has a waterproof double coat, with a soft undercoat and a wiry topcoat.

Airedale Terrier

Tiny but tough!

The Yorkshire terrier is one of the smallest dog breeds in the world. Yorkshire terriers are bold, brave and mischievous!

Utility dogs

Some of the oldest dog breeds do not fit into a neat group that describes their purpose. Over the years, they have been bred to do lots of different things.

A Bulldog's coat is short and smooth.

Bulldogs have strong, thick shoulders.

Bulldogs have short legs but can move very quickly.

The Bulldog looks fearless and is tough and brave. It originally provided entertainment by fighting bulls. Later on, it fought other dogs.

Bulldog

Curly chaser

Poodles were bred to chase birds out of water so that the hunter could shoot them. They have a single coat of very curly hair.

Horse and dog

Dalmatians used to run alongside horse-drawn coaches. They are athletic dogs that can keep running for a long time.

Black tongue

The Chow-Chow was developed in Mongolia about 4,000 years ago. It has a very thick double coat, and a curly tail. It has a blue-black tongue.

Service dogs

People have bred dogs to help them in all sorts of ways. Some dogs, such as Boxers and Dobermans, make powerful guard dogs. Others, such as St. Bernards and Newfoundlands, are great search and rescue dogs.

Boxer dogs have strong legs and are full of energy. ———→

A Boxer's coat is shiny and smooth. ———→

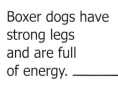

Well-known service dogs

St. Bernard

Bernese Mountain Dog

Portuguese Water Dog

Boxers have strong jaws. Their bite is very powerful.

Newfoundland dogs are excellent swimmers. They are very strong and their webbed feet help them power through the water!

Like many guard dogs, Boxers have a loud bark.

Boxer

Great Dane

Husky

Herding dogs

People use herding dogs to help them control cattle, sheep, goats, or reindeer. The dogs have warm, waterproof coats to help them cope in cold, wet weather.

A Border Collie has a double coat to keep it warm outdoors. ⟶

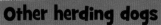

Other herding dogs

Australian Cattle Dog

Bearded Collie

German Shepherd Dog

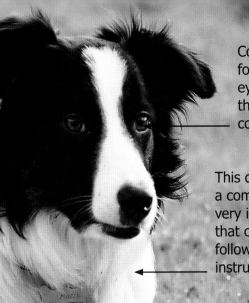

Collies have forward-facing eyes. They use their eyes when controlling sheep.

This dog is waiting for a command. Collies are very intelligent dogs that can be trained to follow many different instructions.

Herding

Herding dogs, like the Border Collie, run around behind the sheep, keeping them in a tight group. Or they stand in front and stare at them to make sure they move in the right direction. Some herding dogs, like the Australian cattle dog, stay behind the animals and nip their heels to keep them moving forward.

Toy dogs

Toy dogs are small dogs that were developed to give pleasure to people. Although small, they still need lots of exercise. Toy dogs love attention and are friendly companions.

Chihuahua

The Chihuahua is the smallest breed of dog in the world. It can be as little as 6 in (15 cm) tall.

Did you know?

Dogs are warmer than we are, so having a dog on your lap is like holding a hot-water bottle.

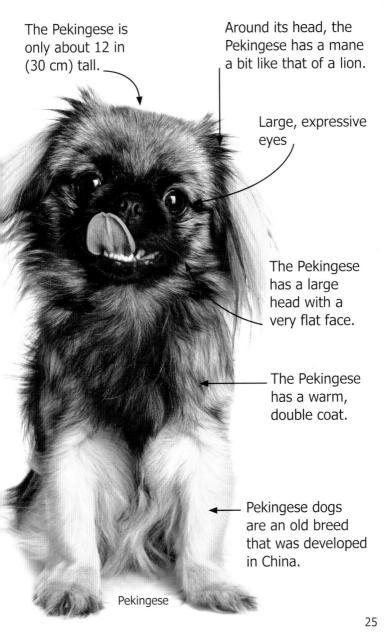

The Pekingese is only about 12 in (30 cm) tall.

Around its head, the Pekingese has a mane a bit like that of a lion.

Large, expressive eyes

The Pekingese has a large head with a very flat face.

The Pekingese has a warm, double coat.

Pekingese dogs are an old breed that was developed in China.

Pekingese

25

Taking care of your dog

Dogs are affectionate and faithful companions and they also provide plenty of fun. They can live for as long as 17 years. Before getting a puppy, people should consider the care that a dog needs throughout its life.

Playtime

Dogs enjoy having toys. They love it when you take time to play with them. A dog should not be left on its own for more than a few hours.

Afghan puppy

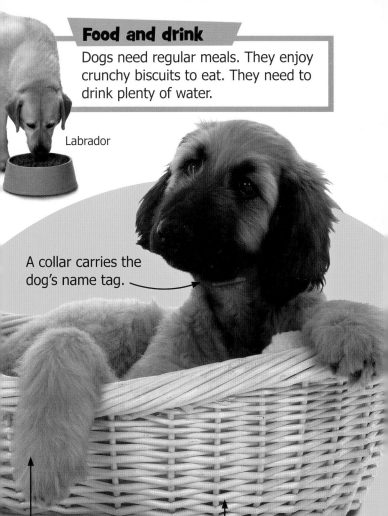

Food and drink

Dogs need regular meals. They enjoy crunchy biscuits to eat. They need to drink plenty of water.

Labrador

A collar carries the dog's name tag.

A long coat needs washing and regular brushing to keep it in good condition.

A dog needs its own basket or bed.

27

Caring for puppies

When puppies are first born, they cannot see or hear and are not able to care for themselves. Their mother cares for them and provides them with her milk.

Playfight

As they grow up, puppies spend a great deal of time playing. This gives them exercise and helps to teach them how to relate to each other.

Bulldog puppies

Crunchy food

When it is over three weeks old, a puppy starts to eat some solid food.

At first, the puppy's legs and tail are both short.

After about nine days, the puppy's eyes open and it begins to be able to hear better.

Glossary

This glossary explains some of the harder words in the book.

breed A group of dogs with particular skills. People developed breeds over many years by encouraging dogs of certain types to have puppies together.

domesticated Animals that have been domesticated live with people and are kept as pets.

double coat Some dogs have a coat made up of two parts, an undercoat and a topcoat.

gundogs Dogs trained to help people when they are out hunting other animals with guns.

herding dogs Dogs trained to help farmers with groups of animals like sheep or cattle.

mane Long hair that grows on the head of some types of animals.

mixed breeds When dogs from different breeds mate, the puppies are called mixed breeds or mongrels.

pack Some wild animals live and hunt together in groups known as packs.

puppy A young dog. Puppies do not reach their full size until they are 12 to 18 months old.

ribs Bones attached to the spine. They curve around the heart and lungs, protecting them.

scent A smell.

scent hounds Dogs that particularly use their sense of smell when they hunt.

sight hounds Dogs that particularly use their eyesight when they hunt.

sprinter A person or animal that can run very fast for a short distance.

tail The tail is a section at the back of an animal's body. A dog wags its tail when it is happy. The tail is also helpful for balance.

terrier Dogs trained to hunt other animals on their own.

topcoat A dog's topcoat is made of thicker, longer hair than the undercoat.

undercoat A dog's undercoat is made of fine hair that keeps the dog warm.

utility Something that is useful.